ONE TO ONE
Glimpses of
Indian Publishing Industry

ONE TO ONE
Glimpses of Indian Publishing Industry

S. K. GHAI

Foreword by
Dina Nath Malhotra
Robert E. Baensch
Richard Balkwill

INSTITUTE OF BOOK PUBLISHING

Institute of Book Publishing
A-59, Okhla Industrial Area, Phase-II, New Delhi-110020
Tel: 26387070, 26386209; Fax: 91-11-26383788
Email: mail@ibpindia.org / ghai@nde.vsnl.net.in
www.ibpindia.org

One to One: Glimpses of Indian Publishing Industry
© 2008, Institute of Book Publishing
ISBN 978 81 207 3789 1

All rights are reserved. No part of this publication may be reproduced, stored in a retrieval system or transmitted, in any form or by any means, mechanical, photocopying, recording or otherwise, without prior written permission of the original publisher.

Printed at Sterling Publishers Pvt. Ltd., New Delhi-110 020.

Dedicated to
Bauji
*My father **Late Shri O.P. Ghai***
who taught me publishing
and to
Publishing Professionals

FOREWORD

Indian book–publishing industry today is one of the top six publishing industries of the world as per the number of new titles published annually. This is a great achievement keeping in view that in India books are published in 24 languages. The major 18 languages have their own good writers and enterprising publishers. Many of the publishers are a one–man–publishing–house and they have been carrying on their work in a remarkable manner, bringing out good books, which have become best – sellers and classics.

This in itself is a tribute to their hard work and initiative and ingenuity. Many Indian language books have been translated into other Indian languages and some foreign languages as well. Though in terms of number of books publishing the national language Hindi leads, but English book publishing occupies a very important place in total Indian Publishing bringing out about 20000 new books annually. English language books have put India on the international level at par with world book publishing. As a matter of fact, English language books occupy the third position after US and U.K.

If one comes to think of the total process of book publishing, it becomes obvious that the personality of the publisher plays an important role. This ingenuity and spirit of adventure lead to making a good publishing house with name and fame. Alongwith the business acumen it is the adventurous spirit and imagination that make a great publisher. Fortunately in India we have such publishers who could have made a great success in any business but chose to enter book publishing and enriched the field. They made star performances and made a mark in book publishing.

It is very imaginative on the part of S K Ghai to do these interviews and have first hand the motivation of these stalwarts of publishing to come into this profession. I am sure this book will inspire many publishers and others also to take lessons from the careers of these adventurous publishers and do still better in their own fields.

I commend this effort whole heartedly.

Dina Nath Malhotra
President Emeritus
The Federation of Indian Publishers

FOREWORD

India is an incredible, complex, huge, and at times depressing country. The basic facts are that India which covers an area slightly more than $1/3$ the size of the United States has a population of 1.129 billion people with a growth rate of 1.6 per annum which represents an increase of 20 million children born each year. The median age is 24.8 years. Therefore, around 36 percent of the population is below the age of 15 or another view would be that every other Indian citizen is below the age of 25. There are six major religions represented by Hinduism, Islam, Christianity, Buddhism, Sikhism and Jainism. In quantitative terms the Hindu represent 81 percent, Muslim 12.1 percent, Christian 2.3 percent, Sikh 1.9 percent and other groups such as Buddhist, Jain, Parsees represent 1.9 percent according to statistics gathered in 2004.[1]

The complexities of this huge population for a publisher are that there are 28 states within seven major regions that speak at least 26 different languages represented by 12 different alphabets. India has two national languages and they are English (central administrative or associate official) and Hindi in the Devanagiri script. In addition to the 26 languages, there are 1,612 dialects. The Indian Constitution officially

---

1. WebIndia123.com.facts about India.1.15.2008

recognizes 22 regional languages while Sahitya Akademi and publishers recognize 24 major regional languages. The single largest "common" language is English which is spoken by over 50 million or 5 percent of the population. In contrast Hindi is the primary language spoken by over 500 million people.[2] It is true that the English language is the single "unifying" language as represented by the indigenous as well as international publishing houses based in New Delhi.

The international publishing industry in general and the top ten global media corporations have been looking at the new and developing mega markets of Brazil, Russia, India and China, also referred to as the new BRIC economies. There has been increasing interest but also reluctance to make major commitments in India. They all have had to recognize that India is indeed very different in that there is not one national language, there is not one national culture, there is not a well established educational infrastructure. Education for a large sector of the population with related literacy is the major challenge facing the country today and tomorrow. The World Resources Institute released a report on "The Next 4 Billion: The Market Size and Business Strategy at the Base of the Pyramid" which clearly defines both the challenges and opportunities in this sector of the world's population including India.[3] The focus in the past has been on food, health and basic industries to meet the needs of a huge population spread over a very large country.

---

2. World Factbook, CIA, Washington, D.C., online data, 2008.
3. Allen L. Hammond, et. al.: The Next 4 Billion: Market Size and Business Strategy at the Base of the Pyramid, The World Resources Institute, Washington, DC, 2007.

In contrast to these macro factors, the publishing industry in India is run by people of the country for their country. They have achieved more than marginal survival. Perhaps they are successful because publishing is a people business that has an added value chain from the author to the publisher to the bookseller and finally to the reader. Each book is written in one of the twenty four languages by an individual who is within the culture of his or her region of India to be read by a very specific audience of individual readers. It is not a matter of confronting the differences but understanding and respecting the differences. Each manuscript delivered to or requested by a publisher is indeed reviewed by that publisher to make the decision to publish the work as a book. It is a very strong endorsement of the fact that publishing is indeed a people business. Individuals within the structure of their society, within the fabric of their culture – make the decision to publish a book and make the decision to distribute a book as part of the added value chain unique to the business of the publishing industry. We can look at the statistics of how many new books are published in which of the many languages each year in India. However, it is still a one-on-one decision between author and publisher and then between publisher and bookseller to turn an idea into a manuscript and then a manuscript into a printed book to be successfully "published" and sold in the marketplace.

Who are these unique individuals who have the ideas to then find the authors to write or who nurture author's ideas to be turned into manuscripts and then into books? Who are the knowledgeable individuals who are part of the rapidly changing country to sense the valid as being different from the transitional or temporary issues? Who are the extraordinary individuals who have been able to combine an intellectual rigor with a financial competence required by the high risk business of publishing? Fortunately, one such individual is S. K. Ghai who as a publisher took the bold initiative to interview fourteen publishers, booksellers and literary consultants to identify what is their unique strength and special entrepreneurship that guided them to be successful. S. K. Ghai provides us with very special personal interviews to allow us to not only get to know each of these individuals but also understand their internal values and state of mind. Here in this volume is an extraordinary insight on how the book industry works within different regions of India. Several individuals have also shared their views with S.K. Ghai on how all this relates to the global arena. These are not reminiscences of the good old times but a dynamic collection of dialogues that reflect the unique character of fourteen individuals that have made and continue to make a positive change in the publishing and bookselling industry and in the culture of India.

Robert E. Baensch
Editor
Publishing Research Quarterly

FOREWORD

It is both a privilege and an honour to have been asked by S.K.Ghai to write a foreword to his new publication, One to One, glimpses of the Indian publishing industry.

I first met Ghai during a copyright and intellectual property workshop held in New Delhi in February 2007, and jointly organised by the Federation of Indian Publishers and the World Intellectual Property Organization. The warm welcome and generous hospitality I received on that occasion from Ghai and his colleagues has stayed with me, and it has been a pleasure now to read the compelling selection of interviews in One to One, all of them previously published in Publishing Today.

What comes across most strongly from this fascinating collection of fourteen interviews with some of the leading names in Indian publishing is the passion and professionalism of the people dedicated to the growth and prosperity of a vital cultural industry. And it is not just a national or domestic picture: several writers emphasise the importance of a global approach, with regular attendance at the book fairs in Frankfurt, Paris and London, and translations of their publications regularly in ten or more national and international languages.

These pieces would repay study by any world publisher. For in them there is much wisdom, a wealth of experience, and a sense of many battles fought and won — the building of infrastructure; convincing government to be supportive (and tax regimes to be less punitive); and carving out sizeable new markets (rather than just niches) from what traditionally had been a rather lazy and complacent 'western'-dominated marketplace.

Many phrases full of humour and good advice stand out from the book. I particularly liked the counsel of Hemu Ramaiah of the Landmark group who says: 'Follow your heart, take calculated risks, and always "listen" to learn…'. Even more telling is Ashok Chopra of Hay House who says: 'It's better to try, and risk failure, than not to try, *and ensure it.*' As far as author-publisher relations are concerned, Narendra Kumar hits the nail on the head with his advice that 'a close relationship [between an author and a publisher] is a good thing, but not an intimate one.' I agreed with Urvashi Butalia's view that 'publishing is fun'; also, that it brings young people the opportunity to learn and to be in touch. V.K. Karthika's belief that 'the biggest bonus in publishing is the opportunity one gets to work with such inspiring personalities' also struck a chord.

Perhaps the last word should go to the distinguished veteran, Vishwanath Malhotra, whose publishing career began in 1937. His is the last piece in the book, and he describes eloquently the post-partition work he and colleagues did in the late 1940s: establishing the concept of copyright; building the importance of national and international book fairs; and the formation of publisher associations. He ends by saying: 'Publishing is a creative business. Enjoy what you do. The business of publishing can enrich your life in many ways.' All three sentiments have informed and guided my much briefer publishing career, and the truths he brings out are both enduring and universal.

January 2008

Richard Balkwill*
COPYTRAIN, Oxford

---

* Copyright and intellectual property consultant to the publishing industry. Associate consultant for the Oxford International Centre for publishing Studies at Oxford Brookes University.
COPYTRAIN: a writing, training and copyright service for publishers.
Pitts, Lower End, Great Milton
Oxford OX 44 7NF
Tel and Fax: 01844 279345
Mobile: 07850924538

PREFACE

The Indian publishing industry has finally come of age. Indian authors have been receiving high acclaim at the International level for quite some time now and their books are a huge rage with the international readers.

Education in India has also spread its wings in each and every part of the country. We have more than 1.20 million schools, 20,000 colleges and 343 Universities. India has a unique position, perhaps the only one in the world, where publishing is being done in 24 languages, resulting in an immense growth in language publishing and in its distribution network.

Book fairs and book exhibitions are increasingly being held in both rural as well as urban India. Every city worth its name is holding these events regularly. Educational institutions too are encouraging book exhibitions at their PTA meetings, annual days, sports days etc., and such events result in increasing as well as creating a healthy reading habits in children, students and adults.

The retail space has increased many folds in the last 5 years and will continue to increase rapidly in the coming years due to the arrival of shopping malls in major metros, state capitals, and big and small towns in the country. This has certainly given an impetus to the display of books, book publishers, distributors, and all those connected with the industry. All these factors have made the Indian book industry a rapidly developing and exuberant industry.

Also the standards of production are at par with the world market, which has prompted many multinationals to begin their operations in India too. India's potential as a partner in the world market cannot be ignored and this will be luring more and more multinationals in the near future.

Even though the industry is going through this very healthy and prosperous phase, there exists a vacuum within the industry in sharing information and ideas. Individual publishers are doing a remarkable job and this is the reason why the industry has been getting attention from the media and has been able to release and make bestsellers. What is missing is a common platform for the publishing professionals to interact with each other regarding issues concerning them.

Keeping this in mind, in Dec 2006 I started *Publishing Today*, an e-journal, which serves as a forum for publishing professionals as well as others to share information and exchange views. In every issue I try to include an interview of a publishing professional and news about the industry. Most of the professionals interviewed by me have been very forthcoming in sharing their experiences and this excellent response has kept me going as I have known them since decades.

In January 2007, I interviewed Tejeshwar Singh when he retired as Managing Director, Sage and became its Chairman; he passed away unexpectedly in December 2007.

Having interviewed such distinguished personalities over a period of time my wish to share their experiences with a wider audience took the shape of a book. A book which would be helpful to budding professionals and new entrants in widening their vision about the industry. The need to compile these inspiring interviews into a book format arose because I felt that their span was being limited due to their accessibility being available to only a scattered few and also because many publishers would rather enjoy a printed book than surf online.

I am very grateful to all the professionals whom I interviewed in the year gone by and their wholehearted support in this venture.

I am also greatful to uncle D.N. Malhotra, Prof. Robert Baensch and Richard Balkwill for writing foreword at a short notice to the book.

1st February, 2008

S.K. Ghai

CONTENTS

Foreword by Dina Nath Malhotra   vii
Foreword by Robert E. Baensch   ix
Foreword by Richard Balkwill   xiii
Preface   xvi

1. **Ashok Chopra**   1
   A good book is like good sex

2. **Hemu Ramaiah**   8
   Follow your heart and always 'listen' to learn

3. **Mita Kapur**   13
   Translations are the next big thing

4. **Narendra Kumar**   19
   It was sheer romance with publishing

5. **Om Arora**   24
   Book distribution is the best business

6. **Pramod Kapoor**   28
   The future lies in going global

7. **Ravi D.C.**   32
   Joined the book industry because of my passion for books

8. **Ravi Shankar**   42
   The Panchatantra is an all time bestseller

9.	S. Anand The real challenge is to make a social cause commercially viable	48
10.	Tejeshwar Singh The art of publishign is dissemination	52
11.	Thomas Abraham From Parle soft drink to Hachette India	57
12.	Urvashi Butalia Publishing is fun	63
13.	V.K. Karthika Publishing is all I want to do	68
14.	Vishwanath Malhotra Publishing is a creative business	71
	Contacts	77
	Index	78

ASHOK CHOPRA
Managing Director, Hay House, India

A well-known name in the Indian publishing scene • Has arguably occupied some of the hottest seats of the Indian book Industry – Chief Executive of HarperCollins India, Executive Director and Publisher of the India Today Book Club and Books Today, Publishing Director of UBS, Vice President of Macmillan India and Executive Editor of Vikas Publishing House • Is on the Board of some of the leading educational institutions.

A good book is like good sex

I have always wondered as to why are you so elusive... you don't attend social evenings, one never sees you even at any publishing event, no book launches or federation meetings. In fact, I had to try thrice before you agreed to this talk. Is it some sort of cultivated image or just, as somebody said "snobbery"?

(smiles) I know Khushwant said that but it's nothing of the sort. I am just a poor manager of time. There are only 24 hours in a day and I try and fit in the maximum as per my priorities.

You started as a journalist then what made you get into publishing?

I had no choice. I got thrown out when I was with the *Indian Express*. And just then Narendra Kumar gave me a break in Vikas Publishing House. It was a very eventful and exciting phase of my life and I enjoyed every moment of it. I fell in love and that affair is still carrying on. It's been an unending romance. Sheer *nasha!*

You are perhaps the only one I know who has started the maximum number of big publishing houses and projects in India. Can you tell us something about them?

There isn't much to say. It's all history. Why think about yesterday? Let's talk about today.

Why? Is there any regret somewhere?

Oh no. Not at all! Look at those projects today and where they are? Macmillan in the north, the UBS publishing list, The Book Club? Look at HarperCollins? How well it is doing today. Ask them and they will tell you what healthy a state it was in when I took over and when I left. It's all there on record. Of course, this was not only my work. I have always been lucky to have a great set of colleagues and each one of them have contributed immensely. But, one just can't sit and keep thinking about what I did in the past. There is so much to do today.

What about the Film Comics project you had started with the Hindustan Times?

It was a disaster. It failed miserably. But, I have no regrets. At least, I tried it. It's better to try and risk failure than not try and ensure it.

I remember that you were the one who started the concept of corporate houses sponsoring books and bringing in socially relevant advertising into books. Can you share your experience with us?

Yes, I did work on a number of big projects with many corporate houses way back in the eighties—Tata, Nestle, Samsung, Hindustan Times, Sriram Group, Godrej to name a few. It helped create a larger print run – and as you know, larger the print run lower is the unit cost. So books were priced low and sales jumped. The authors too earned well. Similarly, the idea of bringing in ads – all socially relevant like anti-smoking and publishing them on the end-papers of books was something that brought down the investments hugely, and we were able to put in that money into advertising and publicity. Remember the large hoardings that were put up in the metros for Nani

A. Palkhivala's We the Nation and what a bestseller it became? I don't think anything like that was ever tried before or after.

So why not do it again?

No, you can't. One does not go backwards in life. You have to move on. Come up with newer ideas. That was relevant and affordable at that time. Now, one has to do something different, something more radical. There is a huge book buying population in small towns of India. One has to reach it....

It is said that Khushwant Singh and Nani Palkhivala have been your godfathers. Is that true?

Palkhivala was certainly my godfather. But Khushwant Singh is my GOD, whom I worship every morning. Both played a very silent but vital role in my life and for making me what I am today.

And in the book trade Om Arora is your best friend?

Who said that? Om is not a friend. He is an elder family member – an elder brother, a *humsaya*, very protective towards me – who, over the years, has always been there for me, though I can't say I have been there for him ever. He is the one I turn to for everything and anything. He is a *badshah*, who lives life king-size. I have learnt from him how to live, and live well!

You have worked for some of the top names like Kuldip Nayar, K.K. Birla, Aroon Purie, Narendra Kumar, C. M. Chawla and S. G. Wasani. How would you rate them?

I hardly knew K. K. Birla as I must have met him half a dozen times and that too at very formal meetings. As for the others, I have very good relations with all of them even today. From Narendra Kumar I learnt what is hard work, S. G. Wasani, whom I admire immensely, taught me the business of running a publishing house, and Aroon was undoubtedly the best boss I have ever had.

How would you explain that?

One never ever felt that I was working under him or for him. Instead, he always made me feel that I was working WITH him. That was the huge difference. Reid Tracy at Hay House is the same. Moreover, even when I made a mistake, particularly during my stint with HarperCollins, Aroon defended me and guided me. Doesn't that speak for itself?

You have published and interacted with many authors, writers and poets. Whom would you choose as the best to work with?

How can I pick and choose for each one of them has been very special in his or her own way, whether it was the top-selling author or a first time one.

You are being diplomatic?

No that's the honest truth. Let's not forget that while dealing with an author you are dealing with a creative mind. At times, even with a genius. You have to handle them carefully and, more important, with lots of respect. True, they have their little eccentricities. But, I for one enjoy them and that in turn helps me handle them better.

I learnt that you have signed some of the best selling Indian names for Hay House. Can you tell us which are the big names and something about their projects?

I can only give you the names of those that have been officially announced, as the rest is somewhat of a guarded secret at present. To name a few, we have signed works of the Dalai Lama, Shobha De, Rajiv Mehrotra, Rohini Singh, Madhu Tandan's extraordinary book on Dreams for the International market while for the Indian market we have I. K. Gujral's memoirs, and *The Empire of the Sikhs: The Life and Times of Maharaja Ranjit Singh* on which Patwant Singh and Jyoti Rai have been working day and night for many years. I have read the first draft and I can say without doubt that it is a very valuable addition to the history of that period. So, it's exciting times ahead for Hay House.

Everyone was a bit surprised with your decision to join Hay House, a totally unknown name in India, particularly when you had other good offers.

No, at that stage I had only one other offer. Everything came later including an offer from S. G. Wasani. But by then I had already said yes to Reid and there was no way that I was going to go back on my word. And it has turned out to be a very good decision. Hay House is a superb group to be a part of, with a great publishing philosophy.

It is rare that publishers find mention in the autobiographies of authors. But many of them have written very warmly about you ranging from K. A. Abbas to Balwant Gargi to M. V. Kamath. And Shobha De devoted four pages on you in her autobiography.

Shobha De has always been very generous with her words. We have had a great working relationship and I am really looking forward to working with her on the new projects.

How does it feel to publish the works of Rohini Singh, your wife?

Like that of any other author. But let me clarify that it was not me who gave her a break. Entire credit for that must go to Rajan Mehra. He discovered her and she did the maximum number of books for him first under the Rupa imprint and then under HarperCollins. Later Pelican in the U.S. signed her internationally. I came into the picture years later, in fact, last of all. It's just that I got the cream with her book *Foolproof Cookbook for Brides, Bachelors and Those Who Hate Cooking* becoming one of the highest selling cookery title.

How would you describe a good book?

A good book is like good sex. It should drain you emotionally and mentally. It's something you can go back to again and again and still enjoy it.

Finally, I know it is a top secret, but can you give me some idea of the book that you are writing for which you have been given this "large" advance by a well-known Western publisher?

(smiles uncomfortably) I didn't even know I could write.

(Publishing Today, January, 2008)

HEMU RAMAIAH
CEO, Landmark Group

Masters in English Literature • Started with Danai Book Shop, Chennai in 1978 and opened a chain of 5 hotel bookshops in the city • Left to start her own bookstore Landmark in 1987 and now have 10 highend stores • Joined hands with East West a distributor • Established Westland-a publishing imprint.

Follow your heart and always 'listen' to learn

How and why you chose retailing of books as your career?

As a child I was interested in books and knew that I would work in the world of books. I did English Literature in college and started working with Danai Book Shop, Chennai as a part-timer. After finishing my studies in 1978, I joined Danai full time and helped them in setting up a chain of hotel bookshops in Chennai during 1978-85. We were able to establish 5 bookshops in 5 hotels.

When you started Landmark in 1987, what were the difficulties you faced in its formative years?

At that time there were no bookstores in India like the one I had in mind. So there was no model to follow. No funding was available because retail did not have industry status. Also there was a lack of human resources with knowledge in this domain. However, this did not dampen my spirits and I went ahead and started the first store in 1987 and now we have 10 stores all over India.

Share your experience as a retailer, distributor and a retail chain organiser?

As a retail-distributor we have much more access to information on new books. This helps us anticipate the market and set trends.

What is your association with Mr Gautam Padmanabhan of East West and how is it going?

As a retailer we were not getting the full advantage of range & discounts from publishers. So we went for backward integration and joined hands with Mr Gautam Padmanabhan, who is the CEO of East West Books and Westland Books, which is a 100% subsidiary of Landmark. This way we were able to strengthen not only our retail but also our competitors by introducing and supplying them the books that sell all over India. It was a perfect arrangement as it helped grow the market. This helped us in our financial growth as well.

We were also able to connect the distributors with the actual readers which was not there earlier. We actually read the key titles and not only the blurbs. Our whole buying team reads and decides what to promote. This way we are able to promote the concept of reading and buying good and great books, through which our market grows.

How do you divide the work between you and your husband?

My husband's name is Jai Subramaniam, who is a chartered accountant and financial wizard. We have worked together for 18 years. He looks after the money which I need for growth.

Now Landmark Group is an established hypermarket retail chain store. How much space you allot to books, toys, stationery and other items when you plan a new showroom?

This depends on the city and the location. However, recently we have opened a 32,000 sq ft store at Lucknow and have allotted 10,000 sq ft to books, which is around 40%, music 25-30% and the rest is given to other categories. However, it is a changing scenario from time to time.

You have created/produced professionals in marketing. How and where you train and recruit them? What do you see while recruiting them?

Most of our core team has been with us for a long time and have trained and learned on the job. It is the best way to learn. We expanded our stores so that we could boost the confidence of our staff by promoting them. Many well known names in retail started with us and we feel content that our team is growing with us.

After the entry of the Tatas in the Landmark Group who calls the shots—you or Tatas?

A. Mr Noel Tata is the chairman of the group. I am the CEO and Tatas have a representative who is the COO and we run the company together. We are working as a team for the expansion which is apparent and are going from strength to strength. Our expansion is quality based and not quantity based.

Any plans of entering into publishing?

We have started with the reprint programme and published the *Chicken Soup for the Soul* series and many other international bestsellers. We have plans for entering into publishing and have appointed Nilanjana Roy as the editor of the Group. She writes regularly for *Business Standard*. Many new titles are in the pipeline.

You said in an interview "supply creates its own demand" and "a recession is a right time to start as it cannot get any worse." Please explain your experiences?

It is a philosophy in which we believe in and time has proved us right. Though in the beginning it takes more time to establish or make it financially viable. But in the long run we grow with the growing reading habits of the people. They are loyal to us and we are loyal to them.

In 1991, the government of India imposed a margin of 200% on imports. Importers started cutting their imports, whereas we expanded our inventory which has paid well.

You got British–European International Standards Certification from U.K. How has it helped?

It has set down our internal controls and standardised procedures across the country.

What is your success mantra for the young entrepreneurs?

Follow your heart, take calculated risks where needed and always "listen" to learn.

What are your plans for the next five years?

We believe in quality rather than quantity so would like to be India's no. 1 retail-distributor, publisher and on-line bookseller.

(Publishing Today, September, 2007)

MITA KAPUR
CEO, Siyahi Literary Consultancy

Journalist regularly featured in media • Director and creative brain behind the Jaipur literature festival 2006-2007 • Literary agent along with conceptualising and directing literary events • Crusader in bringing literature in regional languages to the forefront by ensuring cross-language translations globally.

Translations are the next big thing

How did the idea of starting a Literary Consultancy come to you?

It starts with more than a couple of factors – sensitivity and respect for creativity and the pain a writer goes through while creating a book. If their manuscripts are left lying on a publishers table for a simple reason like lack of time (which is completely understandable), a literary agent steps in to facilitate and fill such gaps. We have talent brimming in our country and as a literary agent I feel, if we could work on each manuscript to create something wonderful by going into the depths and intensities of each book, giving the author detailed editorial and literary feedback, we'd be contributing to the growth of India's contemporary literature. Added to this, was a growing feeling of helplessness and discontent that I sensed among writers writing in the Indian languages – the need to build up on the latent markets for translations as well the need to recognize the power, potential and prowess of literature in our languages – these are our wealth, and to preserve and perpetuate them we must give them a global platform. So Siyahi was given birth to, with a group of us who feel passionately about this – Namita Gokhale, Neeta Gupta, Pramod Kumar, Jaya Bhattacharji, Dr Nirja Misra and an extremely able and proactive team of enthusiastic editors.

When did you start and how is it going?

We started in April 2007 at the end of the month. It's been exciting – reading manuscripts, editing, discussing. I've gained a lot in terms of human value; bonding with some amazing human beings, learning from them. We are working on eight or nine manuscripts right now, three books are being translated and have just got two contracts done; we are a little slow but we are doing so on purpose... I'm not in a hurry.

When do you start working with an author and at what stage? Which are the authors you are representing now?

We accept submissions, read through manuscripts, decide whether we can work with them and get back to the author accordingly. Once we accept a manuscript, we give the author our feedback; thus begins the process and the shape of the manuscript evolves. We are working with Uma Parmeswaran, Anju Kanwar, Shubhangi Swarup, Pankaj Sekhsaria, Jugal Mody, Taj Hassan, Dipalle Parmar, Vijay Lakshmi Chauhan and a couple more.

How does it work commercially?

Commercially, it's going to take a little while till it starts working out.

Do you charge lump sum or do you take a commission on royalties? If so, how much?

We charge the normal rates of commission like all literary agents do.

Any experiences with the authors that you would like to share.

We have shared moments – our authors become a part of our Siyahi family...we bond and have fun working together.

Are you representing the Indian author's internationally or are you only encouraging translation among Indian Languages?

Yes, we will be representing authors internationally – when we talk of cross translations, we mean both – within the country and globally as well.

How many works have you already signed with the publishers?

We have Sampurna Chattarji and Karthika Nair's books coming out with Harper Collins soon.

How would you describe a good book/manuscript?

Well, that's a tough one. I decide on the strength of each, and the strength of each book varies so the deciding factors also vary.

What do you think are the strengths of a good manuscript?

I should feel and sense that the author has lived within the world of his/her book and yet has remained outside of it to give the plot, the characters, the context, the language, turn of phrase and stylistic expression a fair equation. If it is research based, then how deep and intense has the author gone also matters. A lot of it is also played up by instinct... that's why I prefer to treat each manuscript as special.

You also organise annual literary events in Jaipur. How do they help your literary agency?

Till now, I have done the Jaipur Literature Festivals for 2006 and 2007, building them up and directing them with Namita Gokhale and Pramod Kumar, purely as a volunteer. *Translating Bharat* is the first such event being done by Siyahi, with Namita being the Founder Director – with the basic concept being the aim with which we began Siyahi. Translations are the next big thing for the Indian publishing industry. Its time to get geared up and put our best foot forward.

How is the Siyahi Conference different from the Jaipur Literary Festival?

We are different. Our focus is on publishing, on languages, on oral traditions, on understanding copyright issues, on fusing the market forces with the creative aspects, on presenting those areas of Indian literature which are little known, the North-eastern languages this time...we've tried to knit the country together...though the vastness does not permit the knitting to be without holes, we'll fill these gaps by and by.

Are the participants not the same? Is it not difficult to keep up the interest of the audience?

Of the 50 or so panelists we have over packed a two-day conference, only five or six of them are common – publishers like Ravi Singh, Marc Parent, Urvashi Butalia and a couple of other authors – the focus is entirely different, so there is no overlapping and to keep the interest of the audience is not difficult; our USPs are different so there is no worry.

Are you planning any literary events internationally? Where and when?

Yes, we are. We have a couple of proposals we are working on at the moment. Once it is formalised, will let you know.

Are you writing any book yourself or do you only encourage?

I am working on a book...should finish it this year hopefully.

Tell us something about it.

The book is a nonfiction.

Can you throw some light on your journey from graduation to Siyahi?

It is a long story and pretty much conventional...

Does your business affect your personal life?

Hmm, we women are used to multi-tasking. As a freelance writer, my family and I are used to eccentric routines, so Siyahi's work being added on has come naturally with the flow.

(Publishing Today, February, 2008)

NARENDRA KUMAR
Chairman, Har Anand Publications

Joined Asia Publishing House and rose to become its editor • Managing Director Vikas Publishing House from editor and produced a number of bestsellers • Invited to join Delhi Public School as a trustee and became its member education, vice chairman and chairman 2001-2006 • Increased to 150 schools from 20 during his chairmanship • President The Federation of Indian Publishers • Chairman Books Panel CAPEXIL an export promotion body.

It was sheer romance with publishing

Recently the Govt of Italy conferred upon you the title of 'Order of the Star'. What is it for?

I was given this honour by the President of the Republic of Italy, for my contribution to both publishing and education.

You joined Asia Publishing House immediately after completing your education. How, when and for how long?

I joined Asia Publishing House (APH), Delhi in 1962 and was there till 1968 as an editor. It was a learning ground for me. During this period, Asia Publishing House had total domination over the Indian publishing world.

How was the journey from an editor to the managing director of Vikas Publishing House?

It was sheer romance with publishing. Right from the first book I became a central figure in publishing. I was invited both nationally and internationally to give talks on publishing. I initiated the concept of a bestseller in Indian publishing. The high-water mark was achieved with the publication of *Freedom at Midnight*, the biggest seller of all times. *Youth Times*, a Times of India publication did a survey in 1980 for the 10 bestsellers of the decade and surprisingly all the 10 were of Vikas. I left Vikas Publishing House in 1992 after 23 years.

What were the highlights of your stay in Vikas Publishing House?

During my stay in Vikas I went to Bangladesh after its formation and published the *Rape of Bangladesh*. I visited Africa and got the first order of the World Bank from Uganda. We also started paperbacks particularly translation of authors from regional languages including *Cranes are Flying* which was later published as *Tamas*. We also started publishing authors writing on Indian studies from UK, US and France.

When and how you joined the board of Delhi Public School and rose to become its chairman. Tell us something about your achievements and contribution and what role you are playing now?

I was invited to join the DPS board as a trustee and became its member education, vice chairman and chairman from 2001-2006. I continue to be a life member of the board. DPS was restricted to a few places only but during my chairmanship of 5 years the number of schools increased from nearly 20 to over 150.

When was Har Anand started?

Har Anand was started earlier in 1988 so that my sons could carry out the tradition in publishing. They were still in school at that time.

Once you were the chairman of Books Panel of CAPEXIL. How did you help it to increase exports?

I was the chairman in early 80s and they were not considering books separately so I got a separate panel of books and publications created and moved its head office from Kolkata to Delhi. During my chairmanship I took delegations to UK, USA, Canada, Mexico and Australia, New Zealand and Fiji.

When did you join FIP and what were your achievements as a president?

I joined FIP in 80s and was elected its president for 1981-83. During my presidentship I helped FIP to get land for its office from DDA at a concessional rate.

You are a diehard publisher. What is your next bestseller in the making?

I wish I could announce it. Of course you will come to know about it soon. Don't forget that I have returned to publishing after 8 years.

At one time you were considered for the chairmanship of National Book Trust (NBT). Why didn't it come about?

I was invited to be the chairman of NBT in 1986 by Mr Rajiv Gandhi, the then prime minister of India. But, due to some personal tragedy in the family I couldn't accept it.

Where do you want to see Har Anand in the next decade?

I am going to be involved in education again and will continue to be in publishing like earlier. I am working to make Har Anand a global company.

How should be the relationship between the author and the publisher?

I have always wondered whether there should be an intimate relationship between author and publisher. I firmly believe that there should be a close relationship between the two of them but not intimate one. Particularly in view of the fact that the publisher has to deal with hundreds of authors and can't be partial to one or the other.

How would you describe a good book?

Very difficult to answer. A good book should extend the horizons of knowledge and add to the sum total of human experiences.

What are your views on the impact of globalisation on Indian Publishing?

I am very clear in mind that you cannot avoid globalisation in your work and in your lives. The companies have to be either family owned small units or large companies. Middle-sized companies will find it difficult to survive. Like other corporate organisations why can't Indian publishers acquire companies abroad instead of having tie-ups in India?

(Publishing Today, December, 2007)

OM ARORA
Variety Book Depot

With a humble start from a kiosk outside Mohan Singh Palace have a distribution network nationally at Connaught Place, New Delhi • Started a chain of BookCafe's with his nephew and now has 30 stores • Recites Gayatri Mantra when ever he gets time which keeps him in a relaxed mood and positive attitude towards life.

Book distribution is the best business

You are considered a one-man distribution network. What do you have to say about this?

Thanks for the compliment. It is the relationship with booksellers and one-to-one contact with every good bookshop in India that counts. Moreover, I am also in the business for 41 long years.

What clicks – the product or the distribution network?

Always a right product, which I select with my experience.

How was your journey in distribution from Mohan Singh Palace to Connaught Place? Though the distance is small, the journey is long!

My journey started not from inside Mohan Singh Palace but outside from a kiosk of 100 square feet. It was sheer hard work, positive attitude, honesty and luck which helped me all through this journey.

You have worked with your father and brother Subhash Arora. How was your relationship with them and when did you separate from your brother?

It was a wonderful relationship. I joined my father in 1966. After he passed away in 1976, I called my younger brother Subhash to join me. We started Tekson's Bookshop in 1972 and worked together till 1983 and then separated amicably, happily and without any resentment.

Do you buy or sell books from each other?

Yes, we do buy and sell books from each other. We know each other's specialisations and send samples accordingly for selection and purchase.

You started retailing under Book Cafe with your nephew Sandeep Dutt. How is it going? How many stores do you have, and what are your future plans?

We have thirty stores mainly in north India and three in Pondicherry. We are still struggling to keep them a float. We have a strong belief in whatever we are doing. Hopefully it will work.

You have a lot of relations in the book trade. Does it help you?

In business there is no relationship. You have to treat business as business.

What are your comments about other distributors in the country like UBS, IBD, East West, Shree and many others?

I have an excellent relationship with all and we meet regularly in India and at international book fairs.

What is the difference in distribution between now and the time when you started?

When I started distribution, the distributor was the boss. He could sell any book but now the retailer is the boss and he chooses books with great care.

What is the effect of e-distribution?

The effect is not much, as the booksellers/retailers want to see, feel and touch the book before ordering.

Retail space is increasing by leaps and bounds. What are your comments?

It is really great and will increase the business tremendously in the next five years. I wish this development would have happened 15 years ago when I was young.

How do you manage distribution, retailing, publishing and also dabbling in market shares all by yourself?

I have a passion for working and I enjoy doing these activities day in and day out.

Do you do monthly mailing or send representatives? If the latter, how many representatives do you have and what area do you cover?

Along with strong monthly mailing we have four representatives covering Delhi and all over India. We have 800 regular accounts and we do not allow credit till the customer's credit worthiness is established. However, we have the first two or three dealings strictly on cash basis.

How would you describe a good book?

"Which sells well" is a good book for me.

How do you manage to look relaxed, happy and smiling?

Meditation and a positive attitude is the secret behind this. I am in this mood 24 hours a day.

What is your message to the new upcoming distributors / booksellers?

Friends, you are joining the best business, which will have tremendous growth in the coming years. So go ahead and take advantage of it.

(Publishing Today, July, 2007)

PRAMOD KAPOOR
Managing Director, Roli Books

Joined Macmillan as a trainee after finishing education • Started Roli Books in 1978 for publishing pictorial books • Acquired India Ink an imprint for fiction in 2004 • Have Lotus press imprint for illustated books and Lotus collection for biographies and non fiction • Work with Phidon Books as distributor and copublisher for India.

The future lies in going global

Your journey in publishing from Benares to Delhi.

In fact, it was altogether a new line. Of course, my family has an allied line of distribution of paper in east Uttar Pradesh, and my brother had a printing press, where I used to go after my college hours and work as a distributor of lead type in the cases. I started liking this job and after finishing my education, I came to Delhi and joined Macmillan as a trainee. I was given the marketing of higher academic list.

With what aim did you start with Roli Books in 1978?

After working for two and a half years at Macmillan, I decided to start on my own. There was practically no publisher doing pictorial books in India. I published my first book on Rajasthan—fully illustrated with photographs. I had commissioned a photographer for shooting. I stressed on good quality production and printed the book in Singapore. The first print run was of 10,000 copies. Of course, more than 25,000 copies were eventually sold. So that is how I entered into the world of publishing.

At that time there was a need for handling Indian scholarship with skills. I tried repackaging school text books published by FEP Singapore. I packaged them as per the Indian environment/culture and tied up with OUP. Some of the books are still in print.

You are known as a leading publisher of illustrated books in India. How has been your experience?

I am really enjoying the way publishing is growing. In Roli we have three imprints—*Lustre Press* for illustrated books, *India Ink* (publisher of Arundhati Roy's *God of Small Things*) for fiction which we acquired in 2004, and *Lotus Collection* where we publish biographies, non-illustrated, non-fiction. This year we will end up releasing around 45 new books plus reprints.

How was your experience in Frankfurt this year? How did India being the guest of honour country at Frankfurt help Roli?

I must say it was an excellent experience. Germans were not open to Indian literature earlier. But now the scenario is different. Indian literature is largely getting published in German language. I am sure this will be better in the future.

Were you satisfied with the result of your advertising at Frankfurt?

At Frankfurt we promoted ourselves as a premier publisher from India. We even promoted Indian cuisine collaborating with ITC and released a book named *Bukhara*. We were able to tie up with different publishers for co-publication and co-edition.

What are your expectations from the Paris Book Fair where India is again the guest of honour country this year in March?

France is like another home for us. There is no publisher who does not know us. The fair will help us in establishing a good will. It is our major market and many of our authors and photographers are based in France. It is a selling fair. We have booked quite a large stall.

I saw a lot of Phidon books displayed in your office.

We represent Phidon's interests in India. We distribute, co-publish and advise them on the Indian market.

How would you describe a good book?

A good book should engage, inform and provoke thought.

How do you see Roli Books after five years?

Roli is a professionally run family business. My wife Kiran, son Kapil and daughter Priya all are together in this venture. Kapil looks after opening and developing new areas and commercial side of the company, Kiran does administration and Priya makes special illustrated books. They are supported by an excellent professional team.

I feel the future lies in going global. This is what I have experienced and have been practising in the last thirty years. The Indian publishing industry is in for a major growth due to the large addition of retail space and here the future lies in packaging the material for the masses.

(Publishing Today, March, 2007)

RAVI DC
CEO, DC Books & Current Books

Leading publisher of Malayalam Books • MBA from Massachutetts joined family business on his own sweetwill • Publisher publishing 1500 titles a year • Retailer having 30 stores • Distributor and a commercial printer with an ISO certification • Established educational institutions which are highly academic • Started an animation company focussing an animation in science and medicine.

Joined the book industry because of my passion for books

Ravi, I think you are second generation in publishing. When and why did you join it? Was it on your own or by any compulsion?

After doing my schooling and management studies from Boston, Massachusetts, I joined my family business without any compulsion. While at school and college I was actively involved in the Campus newspaper as news editor, and as a bookstore associate. I was active in leading various activities in clubs such as Entrepreneurship club and Economics club. I was also the president of Indian Students Association, the largest club on the campus with over 500 students. I did some successful entrepreneurial ventures while studying.

I decided to join the book industry purely, because of my passion for books.

Moreover, I always considered my father as my mentor. My father D.C. Kizhakemuri started his life as a teacher, columnist and a publisher. As a Gandhian he instilled good moral values in us and his area of interest was the concept of social enterprise and social responsibility. I thought this is one industry where I could really do such activities. Today, DC Books is considered as a cultural organisation of Kerala.

You are all in one – a publisher, educationist, retailer, bookseller and a printer. How do you manage all these hats and what else are you doing apart from this?

My flagship is publishing. Though we are a commercial printing house, we started the printing division to support our large publishing programme. Retailing - I see fun in it. The educational institutes we run are a tribute to my father. Our educational institutions are highly academic in nature and the teaching methods are uniquely designed for competency building. We recently started an animation company focusing on animation in science and medicine.

Tell us about the history of DC Books/ Current Books? How did it progress after you took over?

Current Books was started in 1952 and my father took it over in 1977. At that time it had only 6 showrooms. In 1986, my father gave back the Trissur branch to the son of the founder, Peppin Thomas as a goodwill gesture after the demise of his father Thomas Mundassery.

Now we have 34 stores. 24 stores were started after my joining the business, most of them in Kerala. We have a market share of around 70 percent of the retail of books in Kerala. Three bookstores are going to open up in Bangalore this year itself.

My father started DC Books in 1974. (Prior to it he along with his friends started National Book Stall and co-founded Sahitya Pravarthaka Co-operative Society, which became the model of two success stories in publishing in India). Our publishing activity is based at Kottayam with a brilliant pool of editors in all major categories. We have editors trained at postgraduate level at Oxford University, UK as well as specialists in poetry, mythology, spirituality, etc. We have published many fictions, whose sales have crossed over tens of thousands of copies. Some have even crossed 100,000 copies. English-English-Malayalam Dictionary published by us has sold more than 1.1 million copies till date making it the largest selling bilingual dictionary in India. Our backlist has over 1000 bestsellers.

DC Books and Current Books got ISO certification in the year 2000, and became the first publishers and booksellers in India to get ISO certification.

We have a modern printing unit having mechanised post-press facilities as well. We are acquiring a printing unit based in Cochin to give a boost to our production. 50 percent of our printing capacity is utilised for commercial printing.

We run a residential management institute – DC School of Management & Technology, a fairly large campus with superb infrastructure and intellectual capital at Vagamon. We also run a media school in Trivandrum. As a part of the media school we run Radio DC, a community FM radio from Trivandrum. We also provide training in media convergence, animation and media management.

Just a brief on your father's contribution to the publishing world of India?

My father started the paperback edition revolution in Indian publishing industry in 50s and 60s in Malayalam. His biggest contribution is that he made the Keralites read books. Writers co-operative society, low priced editions, home library scheme, pre-publication sale, book bazaars, book clubs, bookstores in every nook and corner, rural library concept are just few of his innovations and was his active area of contribution to the culture of Kerala.

Many may not be knowing that a sales tax was prevailing across India on books. My father convinced the then Finance Minister A J John to abolish tax on books in Travancore-Cochin state. This was brought to the notice of Jawaharlal Nehru and that is how it was abolished all over India. Similarly he ran quite a few lotteries in 1960s successfully to build a most modern five-storied library in Kerala. The success of the lottery prompted Kerala Government to introduce lottery as a revenue mechanism to the Government. On request from the Government, technical expertise and the machinery used was transferred to the Government. The success of the Kerala Government lottery made the Indian Government to nationalise lottery.

The concept and strategy of making Kottayam the first 100 percent (100 percent literacy in 100 days) literate town in India was conceived and introduced by my father. His initiative was taken up by the district and municipal authorities and was made a success.

He was awarded Padmabhushan in 1999 for his contribution to the nation.

How many new books do you publish every year? What is DC Books' share in Malayalam publishing?

We publish 1500 titles a year, making it one of the largest in the Indian language publishing industry. This figure was less than 300 eight years back. Around 2000 titles are being published annually in Malayalam language and we have a market share of 80 percent in terms of sales. We are among the top five literary publishing houses in India.

Do you have any competition from local publishing and bookselling?

Yes. Stiff competition. But we ensure that we work on our content way in advance, in fact in tune with the reader's choice and trend in the industry. We are known for our trendsetting in the book industry. Technology is also experimented to ensure we meet international standards in publishing. We are first to introduce many technological tools in Indian language publishing. In marketing we use pre-publication sales as a selling tool for many large volume editions, which is really helpful in estimating the future sales. The customers are also benefited in terms of higher discount for pre-booking the copies. Our recent project *Nations of the World* (3 volumes, 2500 pages) sold 22,000 copies at a pre-publication price of Rs. 1500 (Original price – Rs. 2,500) in a very short span. At present, we are one of the five largest literary publishing houses in India.

What are your marketing and promotional strategies?

We run lot of schemes to promote books. We have a huge loyal customer base that pay thousands of rupees as deposit to become a member in our book club schemes. Our author and book promotional schemes have got national attention. When we did the latest book by OV Vijayan in 1996, we released 2000 copies in the first print with 2000 different covers as a painting. We had commissioned a sex worker turned activist to write her autobiography. We got international media coverage for that. The book was discussed by most of the newspapers and televisions. It has already been published in English and many Indian languages. Act Sud, the most prestigious publisher from France, has acquired worldwide French rights for that.

Your major business is in Kerala though it is one of the smallest states of India. What are the advantages and disadvantages?

Though Kerala comprises only 3 percent of the total population of India; one of the three most active reading communities is in Kerala. I can proudly say that my father has been instrumental in making Kerala a reading community. The advantage DC Books have is that it is a household name in Kerala. We believe in co-creation. We work with the readers and writers in shaping our content. We are a respectable brand and we know that our success is based on the content, creativity, authenticity and quality of our books. That is a challenge as well. The disadvantage is that of being limited to one place. (We started online Indian languages bookselling about 8 years back). We are going into some of the Indian languages. Our first dictionary in Tamil will be released in November this year.

How many staff do you have?

We have around 350 people working with us and are mainly from Kerala. We have one of the best team in this industry, committed to their profession. The DC Books, you see today is the result of the hard work and effort put in by our editors as well as the marketing, technical and back office people. The sense of ownership among the staff is really what makes DC Books.

What role as a CEO do you play?

My role is to generate new ideas and I try to bring at least a new idea every day within the system and outside, which is what we are known for. Media companies have imitated many of our innovative programmes. More than anything else I interact with customers and writers.

Our Thursday editorial meetings are where we sit together and plan our content and strategy.

You also organise literary events in Malayalam quite often? Tell us something about that?

We believe that books should reach the customer in various ways – bookshops, book fairs, book bazaars, literary events and directly to their homes. Key success of our organisation is that we are seen as a cultural organisation in Kerala and not as a business enterprise. Author and content-based promotions are part of our day-to-day activities.

You also joined hands with Corner Bookstore, a retail book chain. Who's idea it was and why did you leave them?

Alok Wadhwa and myself started Corner Bookstore. My Kottayam team was stationed in Delhi to start around 25-40 bookstores in the first year, replicating the successful model of our retail stores. The first store was started at Barista outlet at Defence Colony, New Delhi. It became a success in no time. We quickly moved to other locations such as South Extension, Kamla Nagar, Green Park, etc. The brand became quite famous very quickly. One of the reason for our success was that each store was profiled based on the consumer-buying pattern of a particular neighbourhood. As the chairman and majority shareholder, I saw its future in the metros as well as non-metros in India. The reason for my exit was basically, the over enthusiasm of other directors probably adding double the number, which I thought was a disaster and gracefully quitted, transferring my shares in the interest of the company to my friends within.

Does any other family member help you in your business?

My wife Ratheema looks after publishing and scheduling. My mother used to work long time back. But our work place is way different from others. Our general managers, editors, my wife and myself, we all look after various aspects of the business. We meet and discuss things to make the organisation grow. Everyone is aware of his or her responsibilities and there is no need to put pressure or remind anyone about it. Other genre of people finds it difficult to survive in this organisation in top level or middle level.

After all this do you get time for your family?

Yes. I spend quality time with my family. I have three children – Govind (14), Siddharth (11), and Aditya (4). Once at home we don't discuss business.

What is your daily routine?

I do a little physical exercise in the morning. Then I spend some time with kids, and on telephone talking to my authors. I read around 6-7 newspapers, and magazines in the morning. While in town, I am usually at the office by around 9 am. I mainly spend my time on review meetings. I am back at home by around 8 pm. I travel at least three days a week on an average.

You attend every important publishing event nationally and internationally. How do you get time and do you love travelling?

I enjoy travelling. I try not to miss any major international event. This helps me to keep myself abreast with the latest developments both in the national and international arena. British Council had sent me for a training programme in book industry, which really gave me lot of insights. I try to attend IPA Publishers Congress, which happens every four years. Frankfurt Book Fair is something I look forward to every year. I have also been to London Book Fair a few times. This year I visited the Paris Book Fair as part of the French Cultural Centre sponsored delegation from India.

Do you get time to read?

I love reading and cannot survive without it. I do my major reading while travelling.

How would you describe a good book?

A good book should leave something for the reader to take home. Should put the reader into developing one's imagination, and the creative thinking activity widened.

The craft, and the language must be fascinating and something to expand one's vocabulary.

It has to be an entertainer.

Do you have any plans for going public listing?

Not in the near future but I do not rule out the possibility also. May be it is required for future growth.

What are your plans for the next five years?

In the retail front we are planning to open three stores in Bangalore in the coming months. We also intend to publish a dictionary in Tamil and entering slowly into Tamil language reference books. In November 2007, we will be launching our new imprint –*Tumbi* children books for 0-8 age group in English and in other languages. Work has been progressing for the last one year. A management institute in Cochin is also in the pipeline.

(Publishing Today, October, 2007)

RAVI SHANKAR
General Manager, Children's Book Trust

Son of the founder Sh. K. Shankar Pillai India's most celebrated cartonist, he founded the CBT that organises varied activities for children and publish children literature • Now publishes 4 children books a month from one book a year in 1970 • Publishes Children's World–a magazine for children • Patron AWIC

The Panchatantra is an all time bestseller

CBT has completed 50 years of its establishment. How do you look back?

Well, we have made a lot of progress since we began in 1957. At that time we had no building, no printing facilities and not even manuscripts to bring out as books. My father started from scratch and built up an infrastructure which is facilitating our work even today. After passing my school I joined the printing press in 1965. I took 3 months training in production in Germany. Now let me call Navin Menon, our editor who has been with CBT since 1978 to share her experience with us:

> Navin: "It has been a wonderful and creative journey. I began my career by spending maximum time reading children's books and understanding the different concepts and ideas under our founder, K Shankar Pillai. Today I have graduated from simply looking at and reading books to developing story ideas, evaluating manuscripts and editing the same. At that time, when I had joined, nobody was assigned any specific job profile. Each one of us and everybody before us was trained for everything. Shankar made each one of us get involved in everything, so all our learning was integrated. If we made any mistakes he would encourage us to forget and move forward."

My father was interested in printing large quantities and keeping the price of books low so that Indian children could afford to buy them.

CBT was started for entertaining children. How far is it meeting its objective?

We started with the aim of entertaining, educating and providing an exciting time to children while they are growing up. In keeping with this goal, CBT's activities have been initiated. Besides the colourful books we publish to educate and entertain children, the Shankar's International Dolls Museum was set up for children to understand different cultures of the world, to know about the different people and their lifestyle. This is both educating and entertaining. Besides that, we entertain and educate them through our monthly magazine, *Children's World*. We also nurture their talent through literary and painting competitions. Altogether this makes learning exciting and fun. My father's last dream was setting up a centre for children. We are happy the same is now complete. This Shankar's Centre for Children at Chanakyapuri, will be inaugurated by the middle of next year.

How has been the growth of CBT since you became its General Manager?

We have grown tremendously. Earlier we were publishing one book a year till 1970 and now we are publishing 4 books a month. We have established the Shankar's Centre for Children. During Nehru's centenary year we had organised an exhibition titled 'Don't Spare Me Shankar' in May 1986, in Delhi. The exhibits were around 500 cartoons of Jawaharlal Nehru made by my father. Later the exhibition travelled to Chennai, Trivandrum, Bangalore and Kolkata.

You publish children's short stories. Have you not thought of exploring other fields?

All the manuscripts of CBT are developed through an annual competition. We have published fiction, non-fiction, picture books, historical books, teenage stories, sports stories, profiles and biographies and literature on environment and natural history. Some special genres are published in the Golden Set which are largely in four colour, hardbound editions containing short stories, folk tales, scientific and other factual information. However, CBT's short stories are always in demand.

Have you not thought of going into textbook publishing at any stage?

All our books are supplementary readers and it is not our policy to go into textbook publishing. When CBT was started the missionaries were already propagating education through textbooks and there was no such thing as exclusive books for children. What was available were watered down texts of adult literature for children to read. There was a vacuum in supplementary reading material meant only for children. That is why my father made it a mission to publish only supplementary reading material.

How is the Children's World doing?

We started *Children's World* in 1968 and now it has a circulation of 35,000 copies a month. Our Nov-Dec issues have mostly articles written by children. It is one of the leading children's magazines in the country.

Why don't you participate in international book fairs and sell rights of your books? Any particular reason.

We participate in international book fairs through NBT. Many of our books have been translated into a number of national and international languages. However, our focus is more on the domestic market than on export.

Which is your bestseller?

The *Panchatantra* in both hardbound and paperback is an all time bestseller and we have sold thousands of copies.

How would you describe a good book?

Book must be captivating and that make you read more and more.

At one time you had the modern printing unit. Are you changing with the new technology?

We try to change with the new technology and have recently added a four-colour touch screen Dominant printing machine. We have two 2-colour machines and a single colour printing machine with complete binding and pre-press.

How are you associated with AWIC and when did it start?

It started as a writer's workshops under my father. We sponsor them and give all support they need from time to time. They have an office in CBT's premises. They have made me the patron.

How do you feel about having an exclusive Children's Book Fair in New Delhi?

In the year of the child, i.e 1979 we had organised a Children's Book Fair at India Gate. Later on NBT used to organise the book fair at Teen Murti, but we feel that it is better if we have one on a regular basis.

What do you think of the idea of having a separate association of children's publishers?

Why not? Let's have one.

(Publishing Today, November, 2007)

S. ANAND
Navayana Publishing House

Selected for International Young Publisher of the Year (IYPY) award by London Book Fair and British Council in 2007 • Started Navayana Publishing House in August 2003 for "publishing for social change"

The real challenge is to make a social cause commercially viable

When and how did you come into publishing?

The idea was born in August 2003 and by November that year we hit the market with four small titles, priced between Rs 40 to Rs 60 and with extents between 40 to 90 pages. Starting a press exclusively devoted to a critical engagement with issues of caste was primarily the idea of Ravikumar, my partner at Navayana. He is a well-known Tamil critic and writer who is also an activist in the Dalit and civil rights movements. In India, there are independent publishing houses devoted to various political and niche issues: Women Unlimited, Zubaan and Stree focus on gender, LeftWord on issues of the Left, Tulika and Tara for children's books, etc. Yet, there was not one publisher willing to engage with caste—a social reality that affected the lives of most Indians. We decided to address the lacuna and founded Navayana. Navayana refers to Dr B.R. Ambedkar's term for the new empirical Buddhism that he espoused. With the objective 'publishing for social change', we offered a platform for issues most publishers—commercial, academic and independent—shied away from.

How do you describe your list and USP?

We are the first to engage with caste in more than an academic publishing sense. We dare to publish on issues a conservative market would rather avoid. Initially the trade was wary of us, but now they realise our books sell.

Why did you select Dalit literature for specialisation?

That's largely a misrepresentation. We publish mostly non-fiction; our first literary title is out only this year. To talk of caste does not mean talking only of Dalits. Our focus is on an anti-caste perspective. The Dalit movement initiated by Dr B.R. Ambedkar is certainly the major anti-caste voice in India, and Navayana does have a commitment to promote writings by Dalits and a commitment to offer a platform to Dalit authors. However, we are equally keen to engage with Brahminism and Brahmins. For instance, our title *Brahmans and Cricket* is now in its second reprint.

How many books have you published since inception?

We have done 10 titles so far. In 2007 at least six more are likely. Two new titles will hit the stands by the end of March.

Which book has made a mark?

Dalits in Dravidian Land sold nearly 900 copies in three months; historian Dilip Menon's *The Blindness of Insight*, which argues why communalism in India is primarily about caste, has been a steady seller despite being an academic book.

Any outstanding title you are releasing at the London Book Fair?

Namdeo Dhasal: Poet of the Underworld showcases the poetry of the Marathi Dalit Panther poet. The translations by Dilip Chitre, himself a bilingual poet and Sahitya Akademi award winner—are superb. I do not exaggerate when I say this book will place Dhasal in contention for the Nobel Prize for literature.

You have been selected as the Indian Young Publisher of the Year. How did you come to know about this award?

Through a newspaper clipping in *The Hindu*. In fact, my neighbour alerted me to it and asked me to apply. I had earlier heard about British Council's role.

Your message to other young publishers?

I am not so big as to give a message, but I would say the real challenge is to make a social cause commercially viable.

How would you describe a good book?

A good book enlightens as well as entertains. It must be free of errors, well designed and presented.

How do you see Navayana after 5 years?

We are as yet a small organisation with minimal overheads, driven largely by a computer. By 2008, we should be able to recruit at least two editors and some support staff. And yes, Navayana is committed to recruiting Dalit editors. Unfortunately, our publishing industry—mainstream and alternative—hardly makes any concession for social justice. By 2012, Navayana will be a name to reckon with and hopes to sell 5,000 copies of each of its titles. We already have touched 2,000.

(Publishing Today, April, 2007)

TEJESHWAR SINGH (1945-2007)
Former Managing Director, Sage India

Joined Macmillan as desk editor 1972 • Became vice president and branch manager 1979 • Started Sage Publishing House India 1981 • Versatile personality: reading news on National television, which was just a "time-pass" and an actor in the movie Jalwa • Committed publisher and always ready for challenges • Professional in every sense of the word • Man of many colours and a great sense of humour.

The art of publishing is dissemination

You have taken retirement from Sage, when you are still strong to continue. Any specific reason for this?

It is true that I have retired on 1 December 2006 but I will remain non-executive chairman of the company for at least the next three years. Sage was started in 1981 and at that time the laws were very stringent so we had to start the company with 60 percent shares held by me and 40 percent by Sage USA. But now I have sold all my shares to Sage UK and it is a wholly UK owned company – and Sage UK is a wholly owned subsidiary of Sage USA.

Can you throw light on your journey in the publishing industry?

I joined the publishing industry 35 years ago as a desk editor with Macmillan India in January 1972. I was gradually promoted and became successively commissioning editor, chief editor, managing editor, marketing manager and finally vice-president and branch manager in 1979 before leaving to start Sage in September 1981.

Did you encourage your daughters to join the publishing industry?

Yes, I tried to encourage them – we have twin daughters. One daughter straightaway refused – she is a graphic designer. The other one tried for a year and a half and but felt she was not cut out for a career in publishing. She is now a designer.

Was there any exciting event/experience in your Publishing career?

Publishing is never ending and needs continuous attention. However I have one interesting experience to share with you. When I became the vice-president and branch manager of Macmillan Delhi, I discovered that there was a book seller who owed Rs. 80,000. I checked the details with my people and went straight to Chandigarh to meet that person. I confronted him with facts — the books had been supplied to him for an exhibition at Punjabi University, Patiala. He had taken the original receipt from a junior member of the staff on the pretext of making a xerox copy and promised to send the original copy to the Delhi office. However, he never sent it but, instead, subsequently maintained – and rather vehemently —that he had never received the books and asked us to show proof (which obviously we could not).

This was the situation I inherited. However, I succeeded in convincing him to agree that if we could prove that at least some of the concerned books had been supplied to him then he would pay for the whole lot. I came back to Delhi and talked to my friend Dr. Amrik Singh, Vice-Chancellor of Punjabi University, explaining the problem. A week or so later, he sent me photocopies of the bills raised by the bookseller on Punjabi University Library, Patiala, which included at least 30-40 percent of the concerned books. Armed with these bills, I once again confronted the bookseller who, very reluctantly, paid up the long overdue bill.

Another satisfying moment in my career was after I started Sage in 1981. The very first book we published was by Prof. V.K.R.V. Rao, an eminent scholar and economist who had also served as India's Finance Minister. Now how I got this manuscript as a brand new publisher with no books to our credit was because another distinguished academic, Professor. T.N Madan (whom I had known for many years), persuaded Prof. V.K.R.V. Rao to try us out. The title was a great success and we kept it in print for 12 yrs.

Are you still pursuing your other hobbies, like acting, anchoring?

I would love to go back to theatre. Regarding broadcasting, let's see — I would love to work for radio. I would also like to go back to writing book reviews which I used to do regularly for the *Book Review* and the *Indian Book Chronicle*, a book review journal founded by Dr. Amrik Singh.

How is life after retirement?

I am taking it easy and enjoying myself. Now I don't have to go to the office from 9 to 5.

Would you give any tips for the young entrepreneurs in Publishing.

These days the young entrepreneurs have a tendency to take shortcuts to become successful. But my advice would be to remain patient, to stick to your guns and continue working hard.

What is the success formula in Publishing?

The art of publishing is dissemination – bringing books to the attention of readers. If the book is good (content) and price reasonable it will be a success. It will sell. To say that there is no market for Indian books would be wrong. We should not compromise on the quality of books, bring them at affordable prices and be honest to our authors.

What are your future plans?

I will be chairman of Sage for next 3 yrs. The Sir Dorabji Tata Trust has appointed me to monitor the books and the journal (*Marg*) published by Marg Publications, Mumbai, which I will be doing with great interest. I have other plans too but, right now, I just want to take it easy for a bit.

(Publishing Today, January, 2007)

THOMAS ABRAHAM
Managing Director, Hachette India

Started career with Parle soft drink group • Compiled and edited Limca Book of Records • Joined OUP in 1994 as editor but moved to marketing • Executive Director DK in 2000 and moved to Penguin India (with the Penguin Group having bought DK worldwide) as its marketing head • Appointed CEO Penguin India in 2003.

From Parle soft drink to Hachette India

It is a decade long event celebrated throughout the world. I hope you are a witness to the whole saga from the beginning. Please explain?

It is true that Harry Potter books are indeed a decade long event starting from the publication of the first novel in 1997 and ending with the last in 2007. Penguin started distributing *Harry Potter* when Bloomsbury, UK representation moved to Penguin International. It was Teksons I think who distributed titles 1 to 3 in India prior to that. Harry Potter was always a bestseller but entered the blockbuster category worldwide from Book 4 and we were lucky to have the book right then. We imported 30,000 copies, 60,000 copies of title no 5, 1,60,000 of title no 6 and 2,60,000 of no 7. On the first day we sold 1,70,000 copies throughout India. This was possible as the cult following it had, kept growing over the years to the fever pitch it has reached now.

Tell us regarding the custom clearance, security and distribution. How many people were involved?

400 consignments with an approximate weight of 200 tonnes were distributed around 150 locations across India and over 300 destinations – distributors/ shops simultaneously at all locations between 6 a.m. and 7

a.m. Custom clearance and distribution was outsourced to ActivAir, who in turn contracted Safexpress couriers to carry out P-day distribution. P-day security was managed directly by Penguin through Group 4 security agency.

How did you manage the secrecy of the stocks?

Stocks landed in various containers by sea between 5th and 7th July and after the custom clearance was kept at a secluded location in Maharashtra. 25 security guards deployed to keep a watch backed up by CCTV facility round-the-clock ensured no lapses, or break-ins could take place. There was a single entrance and exit point, which had a long walkway before one reached the stock. The walkway had three barrier levels for inspection. In addition to the senior team of the logistics partners, only two people from Penguin – Usha Jha, Head of Customer Services & Distribution and myself knew the location. We spread this (dis)information that no visitors were allowed in its Delhi warehouse until the 23rd July (truthfully) to suggest that the storage location was the Penguin's Delhi warehouse.

How did you manage the logistics of the distribution all over India?

By the 11th the vehicles were on the move to respective destinations in 50 'all weather proof' ISO certified containerised vehicles. These vehicles were GPS equipped with two drivers and one assistant. As an emergency precaution, the complete lot for a destination would not be in just one vehicle. Various vehicles that set out at different times arrived at their 150 plus locations with 3-4 days to spare. Security still ActivAir's responsibility. We also moved zonewise contingency stock to Delhi, Chennai, Kolkata and Mumbai.

Tell us something regarding the distribution within the cities?

With sufficient time margin (max transit time from stocking location to destination was 50 mins.) at hand a fleet of 250 delivery vehicles were used. The delivery personnel were issued mobile phones for direct communication with the delivery heads of the project. The delivery personnel and the drivers of the delivery vehicles had already familiarised themselves with primary and alternate routes after route mapping and mock exercises. Stocking was planned in such a way that the maximum driving time was under 50 minutes. The delivery at the destinations were effected to distributors on 20th night after 2200 hours (online sellers were given a little lee-way with stock being delivered earlier to facilitate individual name based packing) and to retail on 21st morning between 0600 and 0630 hours. G4 had a system of on-location (3 guards at every location) plus a backup patrolling check that would both monitor shifts, check status of each area and report into central control room for replenishments, if needed.

Who all were involved at Penguin in this operation?

Myself, Usha Jha, Raoul Andrews, Ananth Padmanabhan, Somu Sunder Reddy, Hemali Sodhi and Rachna Kalra were actively involved in this operation. All our sales representatives would visit different locations in rotation.

How many copies did you import initially and are you on the verge of another order?

Our initial order was 1,19,000 copies which was enhanced to 2,50,000 copies imported by sea freight. We are ready with the another replenishment order.

How the secrecy of the plot was managed at editorial level and then at printing?

This was of course done in the UK but from what we know, only one editor handled the manuscript and he was in touch with the author directly without any mediator. In UK, it was printed at Clays Printing Press which put up barbed wire fences and had dogs patrolling.

It must have given a boost to the whole Penguin Operation?

Definitely, but we've learnt to treat this as an extra one-off since it leaves a big budget deficit the year after.

How is your language programme going on and did you try for Harry Potter translation rights?

Harry Potter rights were already assigned to various Indian language publishers so we couldn't get any. However, our language programme is going on steadily. We have already released 40 titles in Hindi, 8 titles in Marathi and are launching Malayalam language editions in November this year. We feel that the language markets are under-capitalised especially in terms of distribution and retail networks. We are publishing 30 percent translation and 70 percent original authors in these languages.

How would you describe a good book?

What is a good book? quoth jesting Pilate and waited not for an answer! I can't think of a blanket answer unless it's what a reader likes.

Thomas how and when you came into publishing?

I started my career with Parle Soft Drink Group (later to become Coca Cola) in advertising but since I had a masters in English, I was given the responsibility of compiling and editing *Limca Book of Records*. I always had an affinity for books but hadn't seriously considered it a career possibility. I found I thoroughly enjoyed the work. Later I started looking for a job in publishing. I joined OUP in 1994 as an editor but soon moved to the marketing division on the request of the then MD Neil O'Brien. In 2000, I moved to DK as Executive Director-Marketing and in the same year moved laterally to Penguin India (with the Penguin Group having bought DK worldwide) as its marketing head. I was appointed CEO when David Davidar moved to Penguin Canada in end of 2003. After seven years in Penguin, it is with immense excitement that I look forward to my new role as Managing Director of Hachette India.

(Publishing Today, August, 2007)

URVASHI BUTALIA
Zubaan Books

Joined OUP as production assistant • Lecturer College of Vocational Studies in book publishing in 1978 • Took two year break and moved to UK to join Zed Books in their promotion and marketing department • Started Kali for Women in 1984 for publishing about Women and by Women • Wrote The Other side of Silence: Voices fom the Partion of India *published by Viking Penguin already translated in 10 national and international languages* • Started Zubaan Books independently in 2003 • Published A Life Less Ordinary by Baby Halder working as a domestic help, The book has a tremendous success and has been published in 21 national and international languages.

Publishing is fun

How did you come into publishing?

In 1972, I was studying for my post-graduation when a friend of mine introduced me to OUP for freelance work. Later on I joined OUP as a production assistant. After 2 years I was moved to the editorial department where I handled the Oxford Atlas in Punjabi and Hindi for the Punjab Government who had placed an order of 4 lakh copies. It gave me an opportunity to interact with the State Government department as well as the Survey of India and understand their way of working. I worked for nearly 6 years and then joined the College of Vocational Studies as a Lecturer in book publishing in 1978. In the early 80's I took two years of break and went to UK and joined Zed Books as a promotion and marketing person and to create a women's studies list. Two years later, when I came back to India, I set up Kali for Women – this was something I had been dreaming of doing while I was with OUP and then Zed. Ritu Menon, who was with Vikas at that time, joined me in this when I returned to India with a business plan and a name.

How did the thought of women's publishing come to you?

I was deeply involved with women issues during my college days. I participated in the anti-dowry and anti-rape movements as well. I found that at a time when women were becoming active all over the country, no publisher was focusing on women studies, so I thought of starting a publishing house for developing a list of books by and about women.

You are known for taking up the cause of women authors. What do you have to say about that?

I feel very strongly about it. We have so many excellent women writers, but for a long time, much of their work remained hidden because most publishers felt women's writing was not something to be taken seriously. When we first started Kali, we were often asked why we wanted to publish "only" about women (no one asks publishers why they publish "only" about men!), whether women wrote at all, whether they read books, whether we could run a business !! Today, every major publishing house, and many of the smaller ones, publish books by and about women!

When and how your association with Ritu Menon started and why did it break?

Before I started *Kali for Women* in 1984, Ritu contacted me and we decided to work together. We worked for 19 years. Later on differences started cropping up and we decided to part ways amicably.

How do you feel having become a celebrity after your book The Other Side of Silence: Voices from the Partition of India was published. Was it your first solo publication and in how many languages has it been translated?

I feel good, and I feel grateful. I have coauthored a number of books but this is my first full-length book. It was published by Viking Penguin and has been translated in 10 national and international languages. I did not expect it to be a success, and was delighted when it was.

Which role do you enjoy the most - publisher or author?

I enjoy publishing more though I love writing also. Publishing gives you an opportunity to meet new people every day and to have continual exposure to new ideas.

You are marketing a part of your list with Penguin. How is the arrangement and how is it going?

The arrangement is going very well for both of us. We at *Zubaan* develop the title, discuss with Penguin and then produce. This gives the author the best as the books are printed and reprinted time and again. Penguin promotes and markets exclusively to the trade and we do direct marketing off and on.

What about your balance list? Are you able to do full justice?

The rest of our list is marketed by Foundation Books to the trade and they do their best. We get our payment in the first week of every month without fail.

Do you get pressure from authors to include their books in the Zubaan Penguin Imprint?

Both Penguin and Zubaan get pressure from authors to include their books in the *Zubaan Penguin Imprint*. But we go by merit and try to introduce both new and young writers.

Tell us about Baby Halder's book-A Life Less Ordinary. How did you come across the author?

I was reading *Outlook* in which Sheila Reddy, the book review editor, had written about the Hindi edition of Baby Halder's book. Then my colleague Jaya found a short interview of hers on BBC's web page. I liked very much what the book was trying to do and I tried to get in touch with the author, who works with Premchand's grandson, Prabodh Kumar Srivastava. I spoke to my friends Alok and Sara Rai who are also Premchand's grandchildren and through them I was able to reach her. She was working as a domestic help in Prabodhji's house.

After discussing things with Baby and Prabodhji, it was agreed that Zubaan should publish the book in English but then the question of the translation came up. So I offered to do it and I did. Till now the book has been published in 21 national and international languages including French, Korean, Dutch, Portuguese, Norwegian, Hindi, Bengali, Malayalam, Marathi, Urdu and there is an Australian edition from Penguin Australia, as well as an American edition from HarperCollins USA. The Italian edition will shortly be published by one of the major publishing house, Rizzoli.

You are successful in marketing subsidiary rights internationally. What is the key?

We have learned to do it over the years. You need to know your titles well, and the people you are selling to, so that you choose what you offer, and continue to maintain contacts. We have found this very useful to do.

What is your message to young publishers?

Publishing is fun, and it's an exciting profession. You may not get rich on it, but it's guaranteed you'll enjoy it. I feel more and more young people should join publishing as it gives an opportunity to learn and be in touch with new ideas.

(Publishing Today, May, 2007)

V. K. KARTHIKA
Publisher and Chief Editor, HarperCollins

Joined as editorial assistant Penguin India in 1995 • Groomed and encouraged by David Davidar • Enjoyed working with Shobha De and Dalai Lama • Served as executive editor and rights director at Penguin • Moved to Harper Collins in 2006.

Publishing is all I want to do

How did you enter the publishing world?

I was doing my PhD in JNU when I came to know that Penguin India was looking for editors. I wrote a test, had final interview with David Davidar and after 3-4 days, I received confirmation. I joined as Editorial Assistant. I have been with Penguin for 11 years!

You had worked with David Davidar, how was it working with him?

Unbeatable! I have worked with him for 8 years. He always supported and encouraged me. He was a great boss and that's why he got complete loyalty for himself as well as for the organisation.

How has been the journey in the publishing world?

A. Wonderful! At the time I had joined, Penguin was doing 40–50 titles/year. Now we are annually doing more than 200 titles in English and another 70–80 of them in Indian languages.

Can you recollect any exciting project that you have handled?

A. Many. One day David told me to go to Frankfurt. He believes in throwing one into the sea and letting one learn to swim. I landed in Frankfurt without much knowledge of what I was expected to do. I only knew that it was a trade fair where rights are traded. From that day I never looked back. Now, we are working with various publishers across the globe.

Did you have an exciting experience with any author?

All had been exciting…*(on probing further she continues saying)* if I have to mention one name, it is Shobha De. She is always on the move and there's always something new to discuss! Another person whose books I've enjoyed worked on is the Dalai Lama, through his translators and editors. Not that I am a religious person, but I respect him deeply as a great human being with unlimited compassion!

Any memorable event in your life which you can share?

The biggest bonus in publishing is the opportunity that one gets to work with such inspiring personalities.

Publishing is an exciting profession. Any comments?

I will do nothing else! Each book is like a baby and every day is a new day never lived before.

Any nightmares?

Nightmares are there when you work but can always be resolved if you have supportive colleagues and a mature organisation.

Publishing needs personal attention, does it interfere with your personal life? If so, how do you balance?

There's no doubt that publishing is in many ways a 24-hour job, but since I became a mother four years ago, I've started to try and keep at least my Sundays free for the family. As long as you have a partner who understands and shares the demands of your career, it's only a matter of time management.

She joined HarperCollins India from 1 December, 2006.

(Publishing Today, December, 2006)

VISHWANATH MALHOTRA
Chairman, Rajpal and Sons Group

Joined Rajpal & Sons to strenghten the hands of his mother at the young age of 17 in 1937 • Senior Vice President DAV managing committee • Chairman Lala Diwan Chand Trust which runs schools, hospitals to support charitable social activities • Active in Rotary International for the last 30 years • One of the oldest active publisher in the country.

Publishing is a creative business

You are a living legend of Indian Publishing and we are proud of you. Give us your secret for keeping fit and smiling?

I am flattered by your comments. The credit goes to my parents. I lost my father when I was nine. It was my mother who brought me up and had an important influence on my life. She was active, educated and guided me to live a pious life. Arya Samaj also had a great effect on me. I never got into any kind of bad habits or vices. I devote one hour daily to exercise and walks.

How and when you came into publishing?

After my father passed away, my mother took the responsibility of the publishing house. I joined her at the young age of 17 in 1937 and continued my study along with it.

How was the journey in publishing?

During the pre-partition days the publishing was basically confined to religious and political subjects as textbooks were published by the publishers selected by the Britishers. They used to honour the publishers by giving the title 'Rai Sahib' or 'Rai Bahadur'. We were publishing patriotic books in Urdu and Hindi and the government many a time used to proscribe those books. Our six publications were confiscated. To name a few — *Tarikhe Hind* by Bhai Parmanand and *Massacre of Jalianwala* by Dr Satya Pal, as these books were giving the true history of Hindustan but the Britishers wanted the students to know the history from their own perspective. To counteract that we started bringing out patriotic books to give the true picture of Indian history.

In 1941, during the second world war, I got into the business of supply of books for the fighting Indian troops which gave a boost to our business. Then the partition took place. All our assets were left in Lahore and we started life afresh in Delhi. However, God was kind and I personally compiled 15 Hindi readers which were approved by the government and again established myself in publishing. DN (Dinanath Malhotra) my young brother joined me in 1950 and we were able to publish textbooks for the states of Punjab, Pepsu (Patiala state) and Rajasthan. My elder brother Pran Nath was a prolific writer. He wrote 48 books and got awards for four. He also got the highest award from the UP government in 1949.

In the independent India three things got an impetus. First, the concept of copyright, second, national and international book fairs and third, the formation of publishing associations. We always adhere to the quality in production which is fully appreciated by our authors. I believe honesty is not only the best policy but the best business principle as well.

Our Prime Minister Jawahar Lal Nehru established Sahitya Akademi and NBT which encouraged publication and dissemination of good literature. NBT also started book fairs and promoted participation in international fairs. Globalisation also changed the face of Indian publishing.

Your brother Shri D N Malhotra worked with you for a long period of time. How was it?

Basically I used to handle back office and D N was looking after the important role of public relations. I came into my own after 1975 when we parted company in business.

You must have published books by thousands of prominent authors. Any pleasant or embarrassing experience?

I would like to say that we should respect the authors as they are our ambassadors. One thing I would like to share with you that I had best of relations with the celebrated poet Harivansh Rai Bachchan and we used to celebrate his birthday at my place for years together. Amitabh Bachchan who was a college student at that time used to sing in our house.

Primarily you are a Hindi language publisher but publishing in Hindi has not come of age. Any comments?

I wish I could give a simple and straight answer. In fact, in 1960 the print run of a new Hindi book was 3000. It got reduced to 2000 in 80's and then to 1000. It is a sad commentary on the status of Hindi which is our national language.

How would you describe a good book?

Rarely, does a book come your way which touches you makes you sit up and say – Here is a book which I enjoyed reading and would like to read again.

Now your daughter Meera Johri is actively looking after Rajpal & Sons while your sons are handling Vision Books and Orient Paperbacks. How is it going and what is your role as the chairman of the group?

It is going fine and I am happy with the progress. I feel that everybody should have space to grow that is why my sons Kapil and Sudhir have separate offices and still work together. I am not actively involved and have left everything to them and feel that it is in safe hands. Meera, who is an MBA has become a seasoned publisher in her own right.

How is your influence on the 4th generation coming into publishing?

On my suggestion Sudhir agreed to call back his son Siddharth from US who was doing quite well there and he joined the Orient Paperbacks. Kapil's sons are working in MNCs and are happy with that.

You are also the Vice-President of DAV Managing Committee. Tell us something about your role in that?

I am the senior Vice-President for the past 25 years and involved in policy matters. I take credit in introducing our own textbooks written by DAV authors in all subjects from class 1st to 10th. This has helped me in bringing uniformity, as in all the 475 DAV Public Schools all over the country, students are using the same books. It has also avoided unnecessary corruption and horse-trading. All the books are revised every year and it is contributing to the financial base of DAV, in spite of the fact that our prices are much lower and better in quality as compared to the books in the market.

Are you associated with any social and humanitarian organizations?

Yes, I am the Chairman of Lala Diwan Chand Trust which runs schools, hospitals, social activities and supports charitable social activities in a big way. I am also a veteran Rotarian quite active for the last 30 years.

What is your normal daily routine?

I get up at 3 a.m. and do my reading and writing and listen to music followed by 45 minutes of yoga and newspaper reading. At 10.30 I go to office of Rajpal & Sons and have coffee with my daughter and discuss business matters if any. I devote afternoons to my social commitments and meetings. I am actively engaged in the field of education with the DAV which runs the 700 educational institutions throughout the country. Normally I go to bed before 10 p.m.

What is your message to young entrepreneurs?

Enjoy what you do. If you don't enjoy don't do it, whatever it may be. Publishing is a creative business. Discover creativity and joy in this business where you meet and interact with scholars, writers, poets and artists. The business of publishing can enrich your life in many ways.

(Publishing Today, June, 2007)

Contacts

Ashok Chopra	ashokchopra1@gmail.com
D.N. Malhotra	30, Jorbagh, New Delhi-110003
Hemu Ramaiah	hemuram@gmail.com
Mita Kapur	mitakapur@gmail.com
Narendra Kumar	haranand@rediffmail.com
Om Arora	varietybookdepot@rediffmail.com
Promod Kapur	pk1@rolibooks.com
Ravi D.C.	ceo@dcbooks.com
Ravi Shanker	cbtnd@cbtnd.com
Richar Balkwill	RBALKWILL@aol.com
Robert Baensch	baenschre@gmail.com
S. Anand	anand.navayana@gmail.com
S.K. Ghai	ghaisurinder@gmail.com
Thomas Abraham	thomas.abraham@hachetteindia.com
Urvashi Butalia	zubaanwbooks@vsnl.com
V.K. Karthika	karthika.vk@gmail.com
Vishwanath Malhotra	mail@rajpalsons.com

Index

A J John, 36
A Life Less Ordinary, 66
Actsud (French publisher), 37
Africa, 21
Alok Wadhwa, 39
Amitabh Bachchan, 74
Amrik Singh Dr., 54
Ananth Padmanabhan, 60
Anju Kanwar, 15
Aroon Purie, 4
Arya Samaj, 72
Ashok Chopra, 1
Asia Publishing House, 19, 20
Australia, 22
AWIC, 46

B.R. Ambedkar Dr., 49, 50; Buddhism, 49; publishing for social change, 49
Baby Halder, 63, 66
Balwant Gargi, 6
Bangalore, 34, 41, 45
Bangladesh, 21
BBC web, 67
Benares, 29
Bengali, 67
Bhai Parmanand, 73
Bloomsbury, UK, 58
Books Panel of CAPEXIL, 19, 21
Book Review, 55
Boston, 33
Brahmins, 50; *Brahmans and Cricket,* 50; Brahminism, 50

British Council, 40, 48, 51
Bukhara, 30
Business Standard, 11

C. M. Chawla, 4
Canada, 21
Chennai, 8, 9, 45, 59
Chicken Soup for the Soul, 11
Children's Book Trust, 42, 43, 44, 45, 46
Children's World, 42, 44, 45
Clays Printing Press, UK, 61
Cochin, 35, 41
College of Vocational Studies, 64
Connaught Place, New Delhi, 25
Corner Bookstore retail chain, 39
Current Books, 32, 34, 35

D.C. Kizhakemuri, 33
Dalai Lama, 6, 68, 70
Dalit, authors, 50; editors, 51; literature, 50; movement, 50
Dalits in Dravidian land, 50
Danai Book Shop, 9
DAV, financial base, 75; managing committee, 71, 75; Public schools, 75; authors, 75
David Davidar, 62, 68, 69
DC Books, 32, 33, 34, 35, 36, 38
D.C. School of Management & Technology, 35
Delhi Public School, 19, 21
Delhi, 20, 21, 29, 39, 54, 59, 73

Dilip Chitre, 51
Dilip Menon, 50
Dinanath Malhotra, 73, 74
Dipalle Parmar, 15
Dutch, 67

East West Books, 10, 26

Fiji, 22
Foolproof Cookbook for Brides, Bachelors and Those Who Hate Cooking, 7
France, 21, 30-31, 37
Frankfurt Book Fair, 30, 41, 69
Freedom at Midnight, 20
French cultural centre, 41
French, 67

Gautam Padmanabhan, 10
Germany, 43
Godrej, 3

Hachette, India, 57, 62
Har Anand Publications, 19, 21, 22
Harivansh Rai Bachchan, 74
HarperCollins India, 1, 3, 5, 7, 16, 68, 70; USA, 67
Harry Potter, 58, 61
Hay House India, 1, 5, 6
Hemali Sodhi, 60
Hemu Ramaiah, 8
Hindi, 67, 72, 74
Hindustan Times, 3

IBD, 26
ITC, 30
I.K. Gujral's Memoirs, 6
India Ink, 30
India Today Book Club, 1
Indian Book Chronicle, 55
Indian Express, 2
Indian Young Publisher of the year, 51
International Young Publisher of year (IYPY) Award, 48

IPA Publishers Congress, 41
ISO certification, 32
Italy, 20

JNU, 69
Jai Subramaniam, 10
Jaipur, 17
Jawaharlal Nehru, 36, 44, 45, 73
Jaya Bhattacharji, 14, 66
Jugal Mody, 15
Jyoti Rai, 6

K K Birla, 4
K. A. Abbas, 6
K. Shankar Pillai, 42, 43
Kali for Women, 64, 65
Karthika Nair, 16
Kerala, 32, 33, 34, 35, 36, 38, 39
Khushwant Singh, 2, 4
Kolkata, 21, 45, 59
Korean, 67
Kottayam, 34
Kuldip Nayar, 4

Lahore, 73
Lala Diwan Chand Trust, 71, 75
Landmark Group, 8, 9, 10, 11
Left Word, 49
Limca Book of Records, 57, 62
London Book Fair, 41, 48, 50
Lotus collection, 28, 30
Lotus press, 28, 30
Lucknow, 10

M V Kamath, 6
Macmillan India, 1, 3, 28, 29, 52, 53, 54
Madhu Tandan, 6
Maharashtra, 59
Malayalam, 67
Marathi, 67
Marc Parent, 17
Marg Publications, 56
Massachusetts, 33
Massacre of Jalianwala, 73

Mexico, 21
Mita Kapur, 13
Mohan Singh Palace, 24, 25
Mumbai, 56, 59

Namdeo Dhasal: Poet of the underworld, 51
Namita Gokhale, 14, 17
Nani A. Palkhivala, 4
Narendra Kumar, 2, 4, 5, 19
National Book Stall, 34
National Book Trust (NBT), 22, 46, 73
Navayana Publishing House, 48, 50, 51
Navin Menon, 43
Neeta Gupta, 14
Nehru Centenary Year 1986 Don't Spare me Shankar, 44
Neil O'Brien, 62
Nestle, 3
New Zealand, 22
Nilanjana Roy, 11
Nirja Misra Dr., 14
Noel Tata, 11
Norwegian, 67

O V Vijayan, 37
Om Arora, 4
'Order of the Star', 20
Orient Paperbacks, 74
OUP, 57, 62, 63, 64
Outlook, 66
Oxford Atlas, 64
Oxford University, UK, 34

Pankaj Sekhsaria, 15
Paris Book Fair, 30, 41
Parle soft drink group, 57, 61
Patwant Singh, 6
Penguin India, 57, 59, 60, 61, 62, 65, 66, 68, 69; International, 58; Canada, 62; Australia, 67
Peppin Thomas, 34
Pepsu (Patiala), 73

Phidon Books, 28, 31
Pondicherry, 26
Portuguese, 67
Pramod Kapoor, 28; Kiran wife, 31; Kapil son, 33; Priya daughter, 31
Pramod Kumar, 14, 17
Pran Nath, 73
Premchand, 67; Grandchildren: Alok and Sara Rai, 67; Prabodh Kumar Srivastava, 67
Punjab, 73
Punjabi University, 54

Rachna Kalra, 60
Radio DC., 35
Rajan Mehra, 7
Rajasthan, 29
Rajiv Gandhi, 22
Rajiv Mehrotra, 6
Rajpal and Sons, 76; Group, 71, 74
Raoul Andrews, 60
Rape of Bangladesh, 21
Ravi D C, 32; Ratheema wife, 40; Aditya son, 40; Govind son, 40; Siddharth son, 40
Ravi Shankar, 42
Ravi Singh, 17
Ravikumar, 49
Reid Tracy, 5, 6
Ritu Menon, 64, 65
Rizzoli Italian Publisher, 67
Rohini Singh, 6
Roli Books, 28, 29, 30, 31
Rotary International, 71, 75
Rupa imprint, 7

S G Wasani, 4, 5, 6
S Anand, 48
Sage Publishing House, 54, 56; India, 52; UK, 53; USA, 53
Sahitya Akademi, 51, 73
Sahitya Pravarthaka Co-operative Society, 34

Sampurna Chattarji, 16
Samsung, 3
Sandeep Dutt, 26
Satya Pal Dr., 73
Shankar's Centre for Children, 44; International Dolls Museum, 44
Sheila Reddy, 66
Shobha De, 6, 68, 70
Shubhangi Swarup, 15
Singapore, 29
Sir Dorabji Tata Trust, 56
Siyahi, 14, 16, 17, 18
Somu Sunder Reddy, 60
Sriram Group, 3
Stree, 49
Subhash Arora, 25
Survey of India, 64

T.N. Madan (Prof.), 55
Taj Hassan, 15
Tara Press, 49
Tarikhe Hind, 73
Tata, 3
Teen Murti, 47
Tejeshwar Singh, 52
Tekson's Bookshop, 25, 58
The Blindness of Insight, 50
The Book Club, 3
The Empire of the Sikhs: The Life and Times of Maharaja Ranjit Singh, 6
The Hindu, 51
Thomas Abraham, 57

Thomas Mundassery, 34
Travancore Cochin state, 36
Trissur, 34
Trivandrum, 35, 45
Tulika, 49

UK, 12, 21, 34, 53, 58, 61, 63, 64
UBS, 1, 3, 26
Uganda, 21
Uma Parmeswaran, 15
Urdu, 67, 72
Urvashi Butalia, 17, 63
US, 21, 53
Usha Jha, 59, 60

V. K. Karthika, 68
V.K.R.V. Rao (Prof.), 55
Variety Book Depot, 24
Vijay Lakshmi Chauhan, 15
Vikas Publishing House, 1, 2, 19, 20, 21, 64
Vishwananath Malhotra, 71; Kapil son, 74; Meera Johri daugther, 74, 76; Siddharh grandson, 75; Sudhir son, 74
Vision Books, 74

Westland Books, 10
Women Unlimited, 49

Zed Books, 63, 64
Zubaan Books, 49, 63
Zubaan Penguin, 66

Institute of Book Publishing

The importance of books in the intellectual, cultural and educational development of a country has long been recognised. But it is only in recent years that book publishing has acquired its rightful place as an industry.

Responding to the growing need for professionally-trained and well-honed personnel to feed this growing industry, the Institute of Book Publishing was founded in 1985 at the initiative of the Late Shri O.P. Ghai, who was not only a pioneer in Indian book publishing, but also a visionary who could understand the significance of specialised training and research in the various aspects of book publishing.

The institute runs an annual Condensed Course for publishing professionals since 1986. It gets participants regularly from neighbouring countries, Southeast Asia and other parts of the world. The 21st Condensed Course for Publishing Professionals will be held from Nov. 10-19, 2008.

It also organises short courses and specialised courses from time to time. Now it is developing an Intensive Course on Editing which will be held in Delhi from 4-11, June, 2008. The Institute's Courses are run without any governmental or institutional aid.

The Institute faculty includes academicians, professionals and directors of major publishing houses in India. The Institute's alumni hold senior positions in their organisations.

It has also developed a library containing books on books and various aspects of publishing industry. It publishes *Publishing Today* an e-journal since December 2006.